The Queen Mother
Grandmother of a Nation

Richard and Sara Wood

RAINTREE
STECK-VAUGHN
RSVP ® PUBLISHERS

A Harcourt Company

Austin   New York
www.steck-vaughn.com

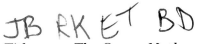

Title page: The Queen Mother talking to World War I veterans

Published by Raintree Steck-Vaughn Publishers, an imprint of Steck-Vaughn Company

Library of Congress Cataloging-in-Publication Data
Wood, Richard.
The Queen Mother: grandmother of a nation / Richard Wood.
   p.   cm.
   Includes index.
   ISBN 0-8172-5715-2
   1. Elizabeth, Queen, consort of George VI, King of Great Britain, 1900—Juvenile literature.
   2. Queens—Great Britain—Biography—Juvenile literature.
   [1. Elizabeth, Queen, consort of George VI, King of Great Britain, 1900. 2. Kings, queens, rulers, etc. 3. Women—Biography.]
   I. Wood, Sara. II. Title.
   DA585.A2 W66 2000
   941.084'092—dc21   00-036933

Printed in Italy. Bound in the United States.
1 2 3 4 5 6 7 8 9 0 05 04 03 02 01

Picture Acknowledgments
The publishers would like to thank the following for allowing their pictures to be reproduced in this publication: Camera Press *title page*, 5, 6, 7, 9, 10, 14, 15, 16, 18 (bottom), 19, 20, 21, 22 (top), 24, 25, 26, 30, 31, 32, 33, 34, 35, 36, 37, 38, 39, 41, 43, 44, 45; Hulton Getty 4, 8, 11, 12, 13, 17, 18 (top), 22 (bottom), 23, 27, 28, 29, 40, 42.

While every effort has been made to secure permission, in some cases it has proved impossible to trace copyright holders.

18.95

Contents

Queen of the 20th Century

Queen Elizabeth, the Queen Mother, is the mother of Queen Elizabeth II. She was not born into royalty. In 1923, when she married the second son of King George V, few people imagined that she would one day be Queen. Nor that she would go on to become perhaps the best-loved member of Britain's royal family.

The life of the Queen Mother, as she is known, has spanned a hundred years of history. For the younger members of her own family, and for millions of others across the world, she provides a visible link with the past. With her warm personality and friendly smile, she seems to stand for all that is best in family life.

Queen Elizabeth chats to occupants of a wartime underground shelter in London, 1940.

At the age of 99 the Queen Mother still appears regularly in public. Here she attends the Trooping the Color with Prince Edward and Sophie Rhys-Jones.

"The Queen Mother is, you might say, the atmosphere of the family. She is so small you could step over her, but she has enormous background influence. When she comes into the room there is a feeling of reverence."
(A clergyman friend, quoted in *The Daily Telegraph*, July 7, 1999)

During her long life, the Queen Mother has met most of the great personalities of the last century—actors, writers, scientists, musicians, sportsmen and women, and political leaders. Many, like the wartime leaders Winston Churchill and Franklin D. Roosevelt, became firm friends. From her place at the heart of the monarchy, she has been closely involved in many of the great events of the twentieth century.

Family Values

Glamis Castle, Elizabeth's childhood home. Glamis was the setting for Shakespeare's Macbeth, *and is the oldest inhabited castle in Scotland.*

Elizabeth Bowes-Lyon was born in London on August 4, 1900. Her mother, Lady Strathmore, had expected to be in Scotland in time for the birth of this, her ninth child. But the baby arrived early. Before long, however, the family was back home in Scotland.

Glamis Castle (pronounced "Glahms") had been the family's home for six centuries. This is where the young Elizabeth spent most of her childhood. With its battlements, conical towers, and resident ghosts, it was a romantic and exciting place to grow up. But it could sometimes be lonely. Elizabeth was close to her mother, who taught her to read and write, to play the piano, and to speak French. Her father, the fourteenth Earl of Strathmore, was a more distant figure whose main interests were crossword puzzles, shooting, woodcutting, and cricket.

Most of her brothers and sisters were older, but Elizabeth and her younger brother David were very close, almost like twins. The family nicknamed them "the two Benjamins" because, like Benjamin in the Bible, they could "get away with murder." Together they enjoyed dressing up, raiding the larder, or demanding treats from the cook, and playing practical jokes on visitors —like pouring icy water over them from the top of a castle turret!

As this family photograph shows, the four-year-old Elizabeth was especially close to her younger brother David, here age three.

7

Growing Up

The Strathmore family was, by any standards, rich. Most children went to local schools, but this wasn't the case for the Strathmores. Instead, they were taught at home until the boys went away to boarding school when they were ten. Elizabeth was in floods of tears when David left. "I miss him horribly," she wrote to a friend. Her mother noticed how lonely Elizabeth looked, and, as an experiment, sent her to school in London for two terms.

Glamis Castle had its own schoolroom, presided over by a succession of foreign governesses like Fraulein Kubler from near Nürnberg in Germany. Lady Strathmore was eager for her children to learn languages, and Elizabeth was soon fluent in French and German. She loved history, especially adventure stories set in the past, and was also fascinated by atlases. In June 1914 she took examinations in all the main school subjects, and passed them all with ease.

> **"I remember that she devoured books, lying on her tummy, with elbows propped against the hard floorboard. She would lie there for hours on end, completely engrossed. Her elbows would be rubbed red raw."**
> (A family servant, quoted in *My Darling Buffy* by Grania Forbes. Richard Cohen Books, 1997)

Elizabeth and her brother David in costumes. Even as a child, Elizabeth enjoyed appearing before an audience and was nicknamed "the merry mischief" by her family.

The Queen Mother still frequently returns to her native Scotland where she spent so much of her childhood. Here she attends the Braemar Highland Games with her family.

A regular visitor to Glamis was Mr. Neill, a famous Scottish fiddler whose long white beard had been worn away from one side of his face by constant violin playing. Neill taught the Strathmore children all the fashionable dance steps of the day. His specialty, though, was the Highland reel, which the Queen Mother danced until well into her eighties.

Nursing the Wounded

On August 4, 1914, Elizabeth's day began with the excitement of sharing her fourteenth birthday with her family at their London home. Her birthday treat was a visit that evening to a variety show at the Coliseum Theater. As the performers took their final bow, the manager walked onto the stage to announce that England had declared war on Germany. The audience burst into wild applause—World War I had begun.

Scottish soldiers resting in a trench during World War I in France, 1915. For Elizabeth, like millions of ordinary people, the war changed life forever.

A few days later, Elizabeth returned to Glamis with her mother and sister Rose. The castle's 28 bedrooms were ready for the usual round of summer guests who went to Scotland for the shooting. But the old routine changed. By December, extra beds were set up in the billiards and dining rooms to accommodate shell-shocked soldiers from the trenches.

The Queen Mother at a Remembrance Day service in 1983. Through her long life, she has never forgotten to honor the memory of those who died in the war.

Despite her young age, Elizabeth put on a nurse's uniform and helped care for the men—many with terrible wounds. Before long, there was personal sadness. Elizabeth's older brothers had all signed up to fight at the start of the war. In September 1915, the dreaded telegram arrived. Fergus was dead, killed at the Battle of Loos, leaving a wife and a baby girl, Rosemary.

"The historic old castle of Glamis Was peculiarly full of green palms, It is now full of soldiers, With bad wounded shoulders, And very bad heads, legs, and arms." (Limerick written by Elizabeth about Glamis Castle in wartime)

London Society

Once the war was over in 1918, life slowly went back to normal. Upper-class girls like Elizabeth Bowes-Lyon "came out" into fashionable society. This was the term for the occasion when they were presented to the king and queen. This began a season of dinners, dances, charity balls, weekend house parties, and race meetings, during which the new "debutante" hoped to meet a future husband.

An American Eye: "*Elizabeth is mildly flirtatious in a very proper, romantic, old-fashioned Valentine sort of way. She makes every man feel chivalrous and gallant toward her.*" (Chips Channon, American journalist)

Elizabeth always enjoyed a mix of city and country life. Here she is dressed for a shooting party at Glamis in 1922.

A debutante arrives at Buckingham Palace to be presented to King George and Queen Mary. As a Scottish "deb," Elizabeth was presented at Holyrood Palace in Edinburgh in 1919.

Elizabeth always loved a lively party, and before long her name seemed to be at the top of every high society invitation list. She spent more and more time in London, where her circle of girlfriends were known as "The Mad Hatters."

One man in particular seemed to catch her attention. He was James Stuart, a fellow Scot, who had not only won great glory during the war (he won two Military Cross medals), but was also described as "drop down dead handsome." Everyone thought they would marry. But James was equerry to the king's second son, Prince Albert the Duke of York. He introduced the Prince to Elizabeth. Albert immediately fell in love with her, and from that moment on, James was out of the race.

Royal Wedding

In May 1920, Elizabeth was dancing at a ball in London when she first caught the eye of Bertie, as Prince Albert was known. Over the next two years, he courted her, proposing marriage at least twice. She was not so sure. Life at the royal court was a daunting prospect for anyone, especially for a girl who was just starting to enjoy the new freedoms available to women after the war.

Bertie's parents, King George V and Queen Mary, were easily won over. The Queen had tea with Elizabeth and her mother at Glamis, where she was charmed by Elizabeth's "poise and knowledge of history." She came away convinced that Elizabeth was "the one girl who could make Bertie happy."

"It's all very embarrassing. I've never been in such demand before and it takes a little while to get used to it. You ask me about my plans, but I can't, you see, because there aren't any yet!"
(The Queen Mother on her engagement)

Elizabeth married Albert, the Duke of York on April 26, 1923. Her wedding dress was made of antique lace loaned by her mother-in-law, Queen Mary.

14

Albert and Elizabeth, the Duke and Duchess of York, leaving Buckingham Palace after their wedding reception. They spent their honeymoon together at a country house in Surrey, England.

On a blustery, cold day in April 1923, Bertie and Elizabeth were married at Westminster Abbey in London. Bertie's older brother the Prince of Wales "grinned like a Cheshire cat" as best man. One clergyman fainted, but the whole congregation admired the beauty of the bride in her flowing dress of silk, lace, and pearls. As they cut the 10-foot (3-m) high, four-tier wedding cake, the couple began their new lives together as Duke and Duchess of York.

A Sense of Duty

As soon as she returned from her honeymoon, Elizabeth began to take on royal duties all over Great Britain. There were charity balls, hospital visits, fund-raising events, society meetings, and any number of parades, parties, and church services.

This photograph from 1931 shows the Duke and Duchess with their children, five-year-old Princess Elizabeth and Princess Margaret Rose, age ten months.

Their new responsibilities increasingly took the royal couple abroad, to Kenya, the West Indies, Malta, and Gibraltar. The cheering crowds who greeted them in Australia and New Zealand during 1927 were inspired by Elizabeth's taste in hats. Thousands of "duchess hats," with turned-up brims and a feather on one side, soon appeared in the stores.

Elizabeth took easily to her new role. But for her husband, it could be torture. The Duke suffered from a crippling stammer and dreaded making speeches. But with Elizabeth sitting opposite mouthing the words, he gained confidence and his stammer became less obvious.

The Duke and Duchess of York on board HMS Renown in 1927 on their way to Australia

"I am quite certain that Elizabeth will be a splendid partner in your work and help you in all you have to do." King George V to his son, Bertie.
(quoted in *The Queen Mother's Century* by Robert Lacey. Little, Brown & Co., 1999)

There were new additions to the royal family, too. Princess Elizabeth, the future queen, was born in April 1926, and Princess Margaret in August 1930. The Duke liked to speak of "we four," and pictures appeared in the papers showing them enjoying an apparently normal family life together. In reality, the young princesses were frequently left in the care of nannies while their parents were away on royal duties.

Family Crisis

The King's broadcast in 1936 was heard by millions of people all over the British Empire.

Edward and Mrs. Simpson became Duke and Duchess of Windsor following his abdication.

In January 1936, the old King George V died and his oldest son, the Prince of Wales, became King Edward VIII. Elizabeth and her husband were soon plunged into a family crisis that was to change their lives forever.

The new king was hugely popular with the people. But he had never married, and enjoyed an exotic social life with a string of glamorous girlfriends. His latest friend was a lively American woman named Wallis Simpson. The trouble was, Wallis was married and had already been divorced once.

People rushed to buy newspapers to read the full story of the abdication.
Many were shocked by the news.

To many people, it was unthinkable for a king, as head of the Church of England, to marry a divorcee. Elizabeth not only disapproved of the relationship, but she took an immediate personal dislike to the "pushy and vulgar" Mrs. Simpson.

Clearly Edward could not have both Mrs. Simpson and the crown. He had to choose. After an agonizing few months, he decided to abdicate and in December left Great Britain to live with Wallis in France. Elizabeth's husband, Bertie, who hated public life so much, now had to become king and Elizabeth became queen.

"Queen Elizabeth may be the nation's favorite granny but she can be steely and even ruthless if there is something she believes in. She certainly didn't want Mrs. Simpson to become HRH [Her Royal Highness]."
(a senior clergyman quoted in *Daily Telegraph* July 6, 1999)

The Coronation and After

Elizabeth's husband became King George VI, choosing the name of his father, a strong and popular monarch. Though she never wanted to be queen, Elizabeth soon discovered a natural talent for her new role.

Despite careful coaching from Elizabeth, public occasions were still an ordeal for the stammering king. Together they practiced walking and talking with crowns on their heads. Elizabeth's crown was decorated with so many gems that it weighed more than 6.5 pounds (3 kg), and gave her a headache. During the coronation, the Archbishop put the king's crown on backward, another bishop nearly tripped up the king by stepping on his robes, and his ceremonial sword belt would not buckle. Despite this, it was a moving occasion for everyone, a first step toward making the monarchy popular again after a rocky period.

The official coronation photograph shows King George VI with Queen Elizabeth and their children.

The royal family at home in 1937. George VI never felt at ease on formal occasions and was happier at home with his family—and dogs!

By 1938, another world war looked likely. The new king and queen traveled abroad to meet allied leaders in France, Canada, and the United States. Many Americans blamed the royal family for their treatment of Mrs. Simpson. But Elizabeth worked hard to win them over. They soon became firm friends with President Roosevelt and his wife, and she charmed one Texas politician, who then told her, "Cousin Elizabeth, you're a thousand times prettier than your pictures."

"Elizabeth wanted to use a knife and fork on her hot dog. Roosevelt grabbed her wrist before that crime could be permitted. 'Just push it straight into your mouth, Ma'am,' advised the President of the United States."
(*The Queen Mother* by Donald Zec. Sidgewick and Jackson, 1990)

War Work

The German leader Adolf Hitler once jokingly described Queen Elizabeth as "the most dangerous woman in Europe." When World War II began the following year, he was proved right. Wherever the Queen went, she brought hope and encouragement, boosting morale in the fight against German aggression. Wearing a flowery hat, three strings of pearls, and a broad smile, she traveled with the King across Great Britain visiting bomb sites and meeting the people.

A woman worker in a munitions factory. Like many other women, the Queen had to take on new roles during World War II.

The royal family and Winston Churchill celebrate the end of the war, on the balcony of Buckingham Palace.

The King and Queen inspect bomb damage in the East End of London, April 1941.

Most people expected that, with London under attack from enemy bombs, the royal family would escape to safety in Canada or the United States. Preparations were made. But the Queen refused even to send the princesses. "They will never leave without me. I will not leave without the King—and the King will not leave," she famously said.

Eleanor Roosevelt, the American President's wife, visited Buckingham Palace in 1942, noting in her diary that the royal family's food was strictly rationed. "We were served on gold plates, but our bread was the same war bread every other family had," she said. The palace gardens were made into allotments to grow vegetables, and a green line was painted around all the baths to mark the maximum depth of hot water.

When Buckingham Palace was first bombed (it was hit nine times), the Queen surveyed the wreckage and said, "I am glad we have been bombed. I feel we can now look the East End [of London] in the face."

Gaiety and Gloom

When the war ended in 1945, parties and public and state appearances started again. Elizabeth was in her element, dancing the conga at Windsor Castle until the early hours of the morning. She began, at last, to enjoy being Queen, meeting people and entertaining friends like the Roosevelts from America. Her favorite party games were "murder in the dark" and charades (when she sometimes wore a false beard), though Winston Churchill, for one, refused to take part.

The King and Queen on tour in South Africa, 1947. On "walkabouts" like this, they were greeted by huge crowds singing.

But the war years had been a period of great stress from which the King never really recovered. "I feel burned out," he often said. Queen Elizabeth did all she could to support her husband, but there was little relief from the constant demands on his time and flagging energies.

One South African told the Queen that he could not forgive the English for conquering his country. Smiling, she replied, "I understand that perfectly. We feel very much the same in Scotland." (*The Queen Mother* by Donald Zec. Sidgewick and Jackson, 1990)

The British Empire was still a reality, and King George felt personally responsible for his 400 million subjects throughout the world. The year 1947 saw the King, Queen, and their daughters on tour in southern Africa. For two months their home was a special white train of fourteen carriages that was a third of a mile long. The visit was one of the highlights of their reign, cheered at every stop by huge, flag-waving crowds.

A Wedding and a Funeral

In 1939, the shy 13-year-old Princess Elizabeth was shown around Dartmouth Naval College by a handsome young cadet named Philip of Greece. They never forgot each other. After the war, Philip, in his sports car, was a regular weekend guest at Buckingham Palace. In 1947, they were married at Westminster Abbey, the bride receiving a hundred extra coupons (clothing was still rationed) for her wedding dress.

The following year, 1948, Queen Elizabeth became a grandmother when Prince Charles was born. But despite these celebrations, this was not a happy time. The King was now seriously ill with hardening of the arteries. Cigarettes and alcohol made matters worse, and in 1951 he was diagnosed as suffering from cancer. The Queen took on more and more public appearances, standing in for the King during his illness.

When Princess Elizabeth married Prince Philip on November 20, 1947, her father said, "I felt I had lost something very precious."

Briefly, the King's health improved after an operation to remove his left lung. In early 1952, he stood on the tarmac at Heathrow Airport to wave goodbye to Princess Elizabeth and her husband as they flew off for a tour of East Africa. He was never to see them again, for he died a week later. The Queen was devastated by the loss of her beloved husband. At the age of only 51, she was facing widowhood and a very uncertain future.

When her husband, King George VI died, the Queen wrote that she was "engulfed in great, black clouds of unhappiness and misery." A friend commented that she looked "like a small ghost."
(quoted in *The Daily Telegraph*, July 6, 1999)

The funeral of King George VI, February 15, 1952. The King's coffin was carried through the streets of London on a gun carriage.

Queen Mother

The day after her father's death in February 1952, the 25-year-old Princess flew home as Queen Elizabeth II. For Queen Elizabeth the Queen Mother, as she was now known, it was a desperate time. She had lost not only her husband and her position as Queen, but also her home. In public she put on a brave face, as always, but her family and closest friends knew how lonely she felt.

The Queen Mother went first to stay with a friend in Scotland. She seemed drawn back to the land of her birth, and bought a ruined Castle, the Castle of Mey, to restore as her home. Some people feared that, like Queen Victoria before her, she might retreat from public life altogether. It was Prime Minister Winston Churchill, a long-time friend, who persuaded her to return to London to help her daughter. "Your country needs you, Ma'am," he told her.

The new Queen, her grandmother Queen Mary, and the Queen Mother at the funeral of King George VI in February 1952

The Queen Mother photographed with her grandchildren Charles, Anne, and baby Andrew.

One of the tasks she most looked forward to at this time was caring for her grandchildren while Queen Elizabeth and Prince Philip were away traveling. But she became a great traveler herself, representing Great Britain on official tours all over the world. She delighted in air travel, and was the first royal to fly around the world (taking the controls at 40,000 feet, or 12,200 m) and the first to fly in Concorde.

"Charles turned to Granny for a shoulder to cry on. During the first years of the Queen's reign, the Queen Mother was both mother and father to them (Charles and Anne). In the full family sense, she took over domestically." (Godfrey Talbot, BBC's Court Correspondent from 1948 to 1969, quoted in *Elizabeth the Queen Mother* by Grania Forbes. Pavilion, 1999)

Meeting the People

When asked to name her favorite occupation, the Queen Mother replied without hesitation, "meeting people." From her earliest days, she always seemed completely at ease with strangers. Whether receiving visiting royalty at grand receptions, or chatting to scruffy children in London's East End, she never seemed lost for a kind word. She has always had a special talent for making people feel valued.

Even on grand occasions, like this parade of military veterans, the Queen Mother finds time for an informal chat.

It was during her tour of Australia, when still Duchess of York, that Elizabeth developed her own special style of walkabout. General waves at the distant crowds were not for her. Instead, she would go right up to a few individuals, shake them by the hand, and speak personally to them. This approach not only left them with a lifelong memory of "the day I met the Queen," but it showed everyone that the royal family had a genuine interest in ordinary people.

Wherever she stays, the Queen Mother likes to meet local people. Here, in her 99th year, she attends the Sandringham Flower Show in Norfolk.

"That was a real swell Queen! Talked to me like she was Mom. She was sure interested in every darn thing, even my old man's stomach ulcer." A U.S. sergeant at an American base in England at the end of World War II. (quoted in *Country Life Book of Queen Elizabeth the Queen Mother* by Godfrey Talbot, 1978)

The Queen Mother's appreciation of humor is famous. When visiting a nursing home in Norwich, England, one elderly patient seemed confused by all the fuss. The Queen Mother went up to her and asked, "Do you know who I am?" "No," the old lady replied, "but if you ask Matron she will be able to tell you."

Colonel-in-Chief

What possible connection could there be between an elderly lady, like the Queen Mother, and the British Army? The answer is that she is Colonel-in-Chief of 16 regiments of soldiers. She does not, of course, go out and fight with them. But she is their chief supporter. She regularly visits and inspects the troops, meets with the senior officers, and attends their ceremonies and special occasions.

As Colonel-in-Chief of the Irish Guards, the Queen Mother "presents the shamrock" on their annual St. Patrick's Day parade.

The Black Watch has a special place in the Queen Mother's heart. This was the Scottish Highland regiment in which her brothers served in both World Wars, so the Black Watch regard themselves as her family regiment. For years she would boost their morale by personally seeing them off when they went on tours abroad, and welcoming them home again, eagerly catching up on their news.

With the Black Watch, her family regiment, in Berlin, 1987. She has always tried to get to inspect them at least once a year.

"She has never been in uniform herself but she would have made a good soldier. She has a great sense of duty and, even when her husband died, she 'soldiered on.'"
(Spokesperson at Clarence House, speaking to the authors of this book)

The Queen Mother often attended the Trooping the Color in London on the Queen's birthday. She always enjoyed the pageantry of the military, which she has taken very seriously. Her daughter Princess Margaret, on the other hand, "stands very regally, though her sparkling eyes will be flirting with the chaps," as a courtier once observed.

At Home

From her childhood at Glamis Castle to her present four homes, the Queen Mother has always lived on a grand scale. Clarence House is her main residence in London. It is full of fine furniture, priceless pictures (including original paintings by the great French artist Monet), and photographs of her husband and grandchildren.

With her daughters at Buckingham Palace, 1946. Earlier official photographs, like this, were always rather formal and stiffly posed.

Royal Lodge in Windsor is where the Queen Mother was happiest. She and Bertie lived there from 1931 until their coronation. "It is grand but comfortable, extravagant yet still very much a family home," says Ingrid Seward, a royal journalist. She also has two homes in Scotland, Birkhall on the Balmoral estate, and the Castle of Mey, which is the only home she owns personally. The others belong to the Queen.

A more relaxed photograph of the Queen Mother, taken to celebrate her 60th birthday in 1960. Here she is shown seated at her desk in Clarence House, her London home.

"She has five or six cars with special number plates, three chauffeurs and five chefs. Clarence House is another world, a time warp. Whenever I go there, three liveried footmen bring in a really full tea." (a visitor, quoted in *Daily Telegraph*, July 1999)

Recently the Queen has made strict economies, but the Queen Mother still spends money freely. The Castle of Mey, for example, costs about $785,000 a year to maintain, yet it is only used for six weeks a year. Some people say that the Queen Mother's debts, amounting to more than $6 million, are hurtful to ordinary people who have to struggle to pay their own household bills.

Elizabeth and Diana— the Generation Gap

When Lady Diana Spencer married Prince Charles in 1981, people compared her with the Queen Mother. Both married at a young age into the royal family from a non-royal background (though their fathers were Lords). Both were adored by people all over the world for their beauty and fashion sense. Both had a real love of meeting ordinary people, a gift which their husbands lacked.

The Queen Mother and Princess Diana watching the Trooping the Color in 1992. Perhaps it was no accident that the camera so often caught them looking in opposite directions.

But there the similarities ended. Diana's parents divorced while she was still a young girl, leaving her feeling insecure. She did not fit in with the rest of the royal family and was a rather shy person. The Queen Mother, on the other hand, had a strong personality, and was never stuck for a witty word. She came from a warm, loving family and her parents-in-law, King George V and Queen Mary, adored her.

With her great-grandsons William and Harry in 1999. The tragic death of Princess Diana two years before brought the royal family closer together.

Diana hoped that the Queen Mother would have plenty to teach her about life as a royal. But she complained that she hardly saw her and that the Queen Mother did little to help her. For her part, the Queen Mother soon came to think of Diana as "a very silly girl" with a poor sense of duty. Over the years the two women, who should have been good friends, came to dislike each other intensely.

Diana said, "She is not as she appears to be at all. She is tough and interfering and she has few feelings." When Diana died, the Queen Mother said to a friend, "Who would believe that she could be even more tedious in death than she was in life?"
(Quoted in *The Last Great Edwardian Lady* by Ingrid Seward. Century, 1999)

A Favorite Grandson

Prince Charles is the Queen Mother's favorite grandchild. When her own children were young, she often had to leave them in the care of nannies while she was away traveling with her husband. Once her daughter Elizabeth became Queen, the Queen Mother was able to spend more time at home and devote the attention she could not lavish on her own children on her grandchildren.

"Ever since I can remember, my grandmother has been the most wonderful example of fun, laughter, warmth, infinite security, and above all else, exquisite taste." (Prince Charles, quoted in *The Queen Mother's Century* by Robert Lacey. Little, Brown and Co, 1999)

The young Prince Charles with "granny" at his mother's coronation in 1953. This picture by the famous photographer Cecil Beaton captures the closeness that has always existed between them.

Still side by side in later life, the Queen Mother and Prince Charles visit the Sandringham Flower Show together in 1997.

The Queen Mother bought magic tricks for Charles from Hamleys, a famous London toy store, spoiled him with toffees and chocolates in the back of her royal limousine, and started playing the piano again to accompany him on the cello. Now that he is grown up, the Queen Mother approves of her grandson's lifestyle—a grand country house and a beautiful garden—and a taste for classical buildings rather than modern architecture.

Charles almost certainly turned to the Queen Mother for advice when his marriage to Diana ran into difficulties. But her advice was probably rather old-fashioned and colored by her dislike of Diana. She has always been strongly against divorce. She believes that married couples have a duty to stay together, especially those in public life like the royal family.

Hats and Clothes

The Queen Mother's style of dress has always been very romantic. Even as a little girl, she loved dressing up, putting on a flowing robe from the acting box at Glamis and grandly announcing "I am the Princess Elizabeth." When she became first the Duchess of York and then Queen Elizabeth, she was able to dress up for real to her heart's content. And she set out to show the world what a true royal should look like.

"I'll never know why she wants all those clothes, as they are all the same. But you won't change her." (Queen Elizabeth II talking about her mother, quoted in *The Last Great Edwardian Lady* by Ingrid Seward. Century, 1999)

Wherever the Queen Mother goes out in public, she is pursued by photographers. Strikingly colored outfits, like this one from the 1950s, help her to stand out in the crowd.

As she walked up the aisle to marry Bertie, people gasped at the beauty of her wedding dress, decorated with antique lace. In Australia and New Zealand, she stunned the crowds with her extraordinary clothes of satin, silk, velvet, feathers, and fur. After a visit to Paris, her dresses and dainty parasols were copied by fashion houses across Europe and America. Even in her nineties, she ordered many new outfits every year, apparently unconcerned by their cost.

Hats were always the Queen Mother's "trademark." As with the rest of her clothes, her hats have usually been brightly colored with the effect of drawing attention to the Queen Mother by framing her face.

But it is the hats that people remember most about the Queen Mother. Her particular style—the cloche with an upturned brim—was developed specially for her by a milliner from Prague, Czechoslovakia. Each hat is made to go with a particular outfit and has a particular name, like the feather-trimmed "Bersagliere" inspired by Florentine soldiers' helmets.

Horses

The Queen Mother's great passion in life—apart from parties and people—is horse racing. She loves the danger and excitement of the race course, the pounding of the horses' hooves, and all the horsey talk with owners, jockeys, and stablehands. Her favorite exercise is to walk around the stables and paddocks where her horses are bred and trained.

"She's breeding to win the Cheltenham Gold Cup in nine year's time," said Sir Michael Oswald, her horse racing manager in 1999, "and I never get the feeling that she's thinking 'I won't be there to see that.'"
(*Daily Telegraph*, July 5, 1999)

The Queen Mother on Derby Day, June 1962. It is a tradition for royalty to attend most of the big race meetings like Ascot, the Derby, and the Grand National.

Whenever her horse wins a classic race such as the Derby, she invites everyone involved to a party at Clarence House. She once threw a party for all the jockeys who had ever ridden for her. "She remembered them all," said Cathy Walwyn, the wife of one of her trainers. "Most of them had retired and were doing other things. But she was able to remind them where they had ridden for her, and when. It was incredible."

Though the Queen Mother attends about 10 race meetings a year, she never bets. Nor does she expect to make money from her hobby. According to her racing manager, "Racing, in her mind, is not a business; it's meant to be fun." In fact, it actually costs the Queen Mother a great deal of money to maintain her 31 horses, probably about $400,000 a year.

The Queen Mother with her horse Braes of Mar at Sandown Park races. Her expert eye has chosen many winners, and over the years, her horses have won all the classic races apart from the Grand National.

Queen of the New Century

On August 4, 2000, the Queen Mother will be the first royal to receive a card from the Queen congratulating her on reaching the age of 100. She has already outlived many of the younger generation of her own family—out of a total of 23 nephews and nieces, only 10 are still alive. She is the only survivor of her nine brothers and sisters.

Leaving the hospital after a hip operation in February 1998

Her stamina is famous. Guests are astounded at how much energy she has and are themselves exhausted by the round of sumptuous meals, after-dinner entertainment, and country walks. "She has house parties every single week for the whole of September," said one of her nieces. "When I've done three weeks of that, I dream of sitting in front of the telly with a boiled egg. But if you've been doing it most of your life, as she has, it just comes naturally."

The Queen Mother in London for her 99th birthday, August 4, 1999.

The Queen had to prevent her mother from going on overseas tours because of the increased risk of accidents. "I really must stop Mummy doing this," she said when the Queen Mother had come back from a tour of Canada in her 89th year.

The Queen Mother has had her share of health problems, including twisted ankles, cracked bones, an operation to improve her eyesight, and two hip replacements. Yet she refuses to give in to physical discomfort. Her ambition is to live to be 100 and to beat Queen Victoria's record of being the longest-living crowned queen. This will, no doubt, amuse her greatly and encourage her to keep active for a few more years to come.

Glossary

Abdicate to give up being king

Aggression hostile attack

Allied leaders leaders of countries that were on the same side in the war

Battlements the tops of walls with openings to shoot arrows or guns through

Chivalrous behaving in a very honorable way, like a knight

Colonel-in-Chief the head of a regiment of soldiers

Conga a popular dance where people form a long line, like an eel

Conical something that is pointed or shaped like a cone

Coupons tickets given for buying rationed clothes and food during the war

Courting dating, going out together

Daunting frightening

Debutante young woman who is making her formal entrance to society

Devoured consumed, eaten up

Don to put something on

Encrusted covered with objects, such as jewels

Equerry a private servant who looks after an important royal person

Exotic rich, beautiful

Fiddler a violin-player, especially in Scottish dance music

Governesses women employed to teach children in their own homes

Morale a feeling of confidence

Pageantry grand, colorful events, such as processions and military displays

Receptions official parties and gatherings

Reel a lively Scottish dance

Regiment a unit of soldiers commanded by a colonel

Shell-shocked mentally ill as a result of being in combat

Stamina natural strength

Steely strong and hard

Trades union leaders leaders of groups of working people

Trooping the Color a ceremony in which soldiers, on horseback, parade past the Queen

Walkabout walk through the streets taken by royals to meet the people

Websites

www.royal.gov.uk – the official website of the British royal family

www.royalinsight.gov.uk – containing general information and photographs

www.gilmer.net/royalty/qmother/information/info2.shtml – another useful but unofficial site

Date Chart

1900 Elizabeth Bowes-Lyon born in London, August 4.

1914 Nurses wounded soldiers during World War I.

1923 Marries Prince Albert (Bertie), the King's second son, and becomes the Duchess of York.

1926 Her first daughter, Princess Elizabeth, is born.

1927 Visits Australia and New Zealand.

1930 Birth of her second daughter, Princess Margaret Rose.

1933 Acquires her first corgi dog, called Dookie, short for "Duke of York's Puppy."

1936 King Edward VIII abdicates. Elizabeth becomes Queen when her husband becomes King George VI.

1937 George and Elizabeth are crowned King and Queen in Westminster Abbey.

1938 Visits to Paris, the United States, and Canada.

1939 Outbreak of World War II. King and Queen stay in London despite bombing risk.

1940 Buckingham Palace bombed by the Germans.

1945 Elizabeth leads the celebrations as the war ends.

1947 King and Queen tour Southern Africa despite the king's worsening health. Daughter, Princess Elizabeth, marries Philip of Greece.

1948 Prince Charles, her first grandson, born.

1952 Her husband, King George VI, dies. From now on, she is known as Queen Elizabeth the Queen Mother.

1953 Moves from Buckingham Palace to Clarence House. Her daughter Elizabeth is crowned Queen Elizabeth II.

1955 Visits America as part of a round of foreign tours.

1961 Carries out duties from a wheelchair after cracking a foot.

1964 Celebrates 25 years as Colonel-in-Chief of the Black Watch regiment.

1970 Scores her two-hundredth win as a racehorse owner.

1982 Prince William, her great-grandchild, born.

1985 Flies on Concorde.

1996 Charles and Diana are divorced, to the disapproval of the Queen Mother. Operations for eye cataracts and hip replacement.

1998 Press reports claim that she is heavily in debt.

1999 Queen Elizabeth the Queen Mother begins her hundredth year.

Index

All numbers in **bold** refer to pictures as well as text.